I0440227

AVOIDING

FLORIDA

FORECLOSURE

AVOIDING FLORIDA FORECLOSURE

AVOIDING

FLORIDA

FORECLOSURE

JEFFREY SMITH

AVOIDING FLORIDA FORECLOSURE
Copyright © 2009 by Jeffrey Smith

ISBN: 1448640687

EAN: 9781448640683

First printing, 2009
Printed in the United States of America

ACKNOWLEDGEMENT

I wish to thank my incredible wife, Gail, for her continued love and support. By urging and encouraging me to share my knowledge of the foreclosure sale process, Gail has made this book possible.

FOREWORD

As a Real Estate Agent and Mortgage Broker in the state of Florida, I know many Real Estate agents. Whenever I have questions about short sales or what might happen under different circumstances there was always one agent I could depend on to give me accurate answers.

Jeffrey Smith.

I know I wouldn't even be selling Real Estate today if Jeffrey hadn't encouraged me, answered my questions, and taught me how to make foreclosures my specialty.

His experience, knowledge, honesty, and desire to help people in the foreclosure situation has been an inspiration to me and I highly recommend this book to homeowners and agents alike to understand the process and take the necessary steps to avoid the stain of foreclosure on a credit record.

- *Mark Galbraith*
Tampa, Florida

DISCLAIMER

Jeffrey Smith is a licensed Realtor and licensed Mortgage Broker. Jeffrey Smith is *not* a licensed attorney, tax advisor, or any other licensed professional.

Nothing in this book is to be taken as legal, financial, or tax advice in any way. This information may be inaccurate at the time of the reading as changes are constantly taking place. Please seek appropriate legal or tax advice from a licensed professional.

INTRODUCTION

It used to be said that the definition of a RECESSION was when your *neighbor* was out of a job. The definition of a DEPRESSION is when *you're* out of a job.

Most of us that face foreclosure (I've gone through it myself) know that there are many different reasons for getting behind in mortgage payments. It's being completely out of a job, temporarily out of a job, downsized in pay (though *they* expect the same output and responsibilities) or just plain skyrocketing costs of everything else. It still boils down to

1. A decrease of income

2. Unexpected expenses or increased outgo.

This book will help guide you through the maze of collection agents, Attorneys, Loss Mitigators, scam artists, "buyers", Real Estate Agents, Mortgage Brokers, Bank reps, and other assorted people that make a profit in some way from your misfortune. I can't even discount myself benefitting, since you paid for this book. If you are a homeowner facing foreclosure, hopefully, you were *given* a copy by me personally or someone else that cares about your situation. If you are a Real Estate Agent, it's possible this guide may add something to your short sale knowledge. If you have successfully closed at least 12 homes on a short sale basis, you already are an expert. I am a firm believer that the best way to learn is by doing. When it comes to short sales, no amount of book learning can come close to the experience.

CONTENTS

Overview

Chapter One

This book was written for you, the homeowner.

If you aren't really the reader type and want the quickest and simplest rundown on what kind of options are available to you, go straight to Chapter 10 – Summing Up.

For a variety of reasons, many Florida property owners are now facing foreclosure.

People have asked me why I've limited my book to just foreclosures in Florida, and the reason is simple.

Florida is the only state I'm really familiar with the foreclosure process. It would be pointless, misleading, and untruthful for me to try to pretend I know all about foreclosure in all the other states as well. Truthfully, I am still learning from every shortsale I do because every transaction is a little bit different and the lenders keep changing their policies.

Fortunately, the foreclosure *process* in Florida is the same throughout the state but, unfortunately, it *is* slightly different with each lender.

The main thing you will learn is how much time you may remain in the home and how much time each step of the foreclosure process will take.

If you want to stay in your home, the absolute best option today is to see if a short refinance is workable with your lender.

The next best thing for *some* would be a loan modification.

In some cases, a "regular" sale of the property is a workable solution.

If selling is the last resort to prevent foreclosure, or if the value of the home is nowhere near what is owed on the mortgage, a "short sale" may be the best solution.

Bankruptcy is a possible option, but in the end the property still gets foreclosed. (unless it's a chapter 13)

A Deed-in-Lieu is *sometimes* better for the bank and not good for you.

The worst option to select as far as both you *and* the bank are concerned is to do absolutely nothing.

Each one of these options has a different affect on your credit.

Each option affects the money (your money) available.

Each option affects the collection process.

Throughout this book, the terms "banks" and "lenders" will be used interchangeably. Many times the company collecting or "servicing" the loan is NOT the same company as the one that has actually lent the money on the loan.

In addition to that, the actual lender sometimes sells the loan to another lender and sometimes when the loan goes into default, the 1st lender will sell to another lender to avoid all the hassles of dealing with a foreclosure in the first place. This process happens more frequently with second mortgages.

This book will guide you through the entire process and the first thing you need to know is ...

What Happens

Chapter Two

As I write this, we are starting the third year of a depression that normally runs in a six year cycle.

In Florida, a good portion of our economy is based on the building and construction industry. This is due to visitors and the elderly wanting to make Florida their "final home." (in more ways than one)

If you are like most homeowners in Florida, you are what is called "upside down" on your mortgage. (You owe more than the house is worth in today's market.

When you've fallen behind a payment or two, the bank collection department starts their calls asking for the money that you would have paid if you had it to begin with.
Next, you will start getting postcards and letters and all sorts of offers to "help." Some of these "helpers" are for real and some of them are not. Sometimes, it's hard to tell the difference. The ones that aren't for real will sometimes ask for money upfront. A legitimate "helper" never will.

It isn't only you and the lender that are affected by your foreclosure but also your neighbor, your neighborhood, and your town or city.

A good thing for everyone is that the lender does *not* want your house.

Strangely enough, the mortgage owed on the house is an *asset* to the lender. If they foreclosed, it would then be considered a *liability.*

There is a tremendous backlog of foreclosure cases that the lenders are trying to process.

This backlog has caused the lenders to hire phone "interceptors." (persons that keep you from talking directly with anyone that can do anything)

The people you will need to deal with are called "loss mitigators" or "loss negotiators" (It's their job to keep the banks losses at a minimum) *not* the collections department. The collections department is interested in only one thing and that is extracting from you any money that they can.

If your home in Florida is your primary residence, there are certain tax advantages.

If the home or duplex or townhouse, etc. was bought as an investment, there are certain tax *dis*advantages.

It's important to know if your property has any equity. Be realistic. If all the homes in your neighborhood are selling for around $150k, *your* home is most likely *not* worth $200k. It is also important to deduct 1% of the value of your home for every foreclosure in the neighborhood. (count any house that has been vacant for more than 1 month as foreclosed)

Just as you had to *qualify* for the loan to buy the house, there is a different kind of *qualifying* for each of the programs to avoid foreclosure. I'll go into the qualifications for each program as we come to it but it is important to remember that the option which you would *like* to choose is not necessarily an option that you can qualify for.

Everything we are going to talk about in this book is about YOU, the homeowner, and the available...

Options and Choices

Chapter Three

In the first chapter, we mentioned the options open to you as a homeowner.

In this chapter, we will be going over *in general* what each one is. In subsequent chapters we'll go into detail about how each one works, and the qualifications for that particular program.

Doing nothing means just that – doing nothing and eventually having the sheriff remove you from your home.

Deed-in-lieu-of foreclosure is the same as foreclosure except that there is less loss to the bank than a regular foreclosure since you surrender the deed to the bank.

A **regular sale** is if you have enough equity to sell your home, make up all the back payments, pay closing costs, pay any other fees (Realtor, home warranty, repairs, fix-up, clean up, etc. and still walk away with at least a dollar or two.)

Paying up is if you should come into some money from whatever source, (relative, lottery, work bonus, etc.) and you have enough to bring your loan current and so you may stay in your home.

A **short refinance** will enable you to stay in your home and have your mortgage payment lowered to *whatever the mortgage payment would be at the current market value of the home.*

A **loan modification** lets you stay in your home but the payment is near or sometimes more than what you were paying before and you still may owe more (far more) than the house is worth.

A **short sale** sells your home almost like a regular sale except that you do not receive any money from the sale of your home. The lender pays all the closing costs, the realtor fees, second mortgage, HOA (home owners association) and sometimes minor liens that are on the property.

In a **bankruptcy**, (except for chapter 13) IF it is successful, the foreclosure on the home is simply delayed.

Each option has different lender requirements and different qualifying (for you, the house, and the market) that must follow the bank's guidelines.

Anyone of the options mentioned above can absolutely be done on your own. (especially deed-in-lieu and doing nothing)

If you are out of work and have a lot of time on your hands, you can get on the internet, study all these options, choose which one is best for you, negotiate with the bank, and spend hours on the phone.

Even bankruptcy *can* be done by yourself (free except for a whole lot of time, research, and filing fees) a para-legal (currently about $800-1400.) or an Attorney (currently about $1400-4500 depending on the type and complications.)

If you cannot do a regular sale and choose another option, almost all have price tags.

Most of your life you've probably had the understanding that the situation is hopeless once the foreclosure papers have been served. The general public thinks along the lines of, "this is it, I can't make up all those back payments. The lender is suing for my property back. Any day now the sheriff will probably come with some deputies and put my stuff out in the street. I better get out now to avoid all the hassle."

The situation is NOT hopeless. There are many options available to you and some do not lead to eventual foreclosure. The important thing to ask yourself is, "What is the best option for me, in my situation, right now and for the long term?"

Many choose to take the easy way out which is possibly the worst option for you *and* the lender, and that is ...

Doing Nothing

Chapter Four

Even if you choose to do nothing, you should know *what* is going to happen with your house and *when* it's going to happen.

Some lenders are right on top of things and give you a call as soon as you miss your first payment.

If your phone is disconnected or you're not responding to their letters or calls, they may send out a bank representative to see if your home is still occupied and if so, what your intentions are.

The foreclosure process will be speeded up if you respond by telling them you plan to do nothing and just let the home be foreclosed.

If you tell them you are trying to save your house, trying to get the money together, trying to work it out with the bank, or considering bankruptcy, this will cause the foreclosure process to proceed at its *normally* slow pace.

When you continue to do nothing, the lender will then issue a notice of default.

In Florida, a notice of default means you have defaulted on the signed, contractual, mortgage agreement on your home. In court, if you don't show up for the hearing, the lender wins by default and a default win is like saying, "I give up. The lender is right. I should give them their house back."

A "lis pendens" will be hand delivered to you by a process server. If you aren't living at the property address and tenants are, they will be served with pretty much the same papers you'll be served with. The papers basically say to the tenants (in a nice way) please get out.

Lis Pendens or code "LP" when looking at online court records, is Latin and roughly means Lawsuit Pending – easy to remember because it sounds like it.

The time frame for this "LP" to be filed varies with each lender.

Generally, you will receive the LP notice anywhere between 3 months after your last payment and up to about 10 months after your last payment.

The "LP" says that you must respond within 20 days of receipt of the notice.

If you're still doing nothing, you won't get in any *extra* trouble for NOT responding within the 20 days following the lis pendens being served. The lender would rather you didn't, since it causes an *automatic default* entered.

After the LP is filed and there is no response from you, you will receive a notice of a hearing.

This notice of a hearing will arrive between 4 and 14 weeks later (if you don't respond) and give a hearing date about 3 weeks away from the time you receive the letter.

The hearing will be at the chambers of a Civil Circuit Judge, which are normally located at the county Judicial Building. It is a "final hearing for summary judgement of foreclosure." The hearing notice will have the name of the judge and what time the hearing is to take place.

At the hearing, if you are not present, the Judge will set a foreclosure date for either 30 or 60 days (approximately) from the hearing date.

The foreclosure sale is normally done at the same county courthouse as the hearing and since the lender wants all that is owed on the property plus attorney, late fees and back payments, the lender usually is the only bidder. (With homes having little or no equity, or reverse equity)

The nominal bid the lender makes is $100 since they are merely recovering property that was pledged to them as security for the loan.

Occasionally, a novice or wannabe investor that misunderstands what is happening thinks they might get a good deal and bids the lender up with a bid of $200 or $300.

The lender then bids the full amount owed and the bidding is over *unless* somebody bids higher than what is owed the lender.

If that happens, (very unlikely in this market) the lender is delighted to get all the money owed. They didn't have to take possession of the property, and you are off the hook for any deficiency, since there is none.

After the foreclosure takes place, regardless of who the winning bidder was, you have ten days to vacate the property. (or redeem it if you should win the lottery)

After the ten days are up, the lender sends out a representative (usually a Realtor) to check for occupancy and condition of the property. This Realtor is usually the one that is going to be given the listing from the lender and told to put a price on the house that will get it sold in

30, 60, or 90 days. Sometimes the lender asks the realtor to tell them what they think it will sell for at each of the 30,60 or 90 day times.

If you are STILL in the property you *might* be offered a deal called "cash for keys."

If you agree to vacate the premises within a week to ten days, AND leave nothing behind AND swept clean, AND do no destruction to the property, you MAY be offered $500-1500. for your co-operation. Any appliances taken or damage done will increase the size of the deficiency judgement against you.

Of course, the lenders rep will not give you any money in advance but *will* give it to you after satisfactory completion.

Probably the best solution of all the options available (with home values about 50-55% of what they were at their peak) *if it's possible in your particular situation,* is a ...

Short Refinance

Chapter Five

A short refinance is a little complicated for those that don't work in this field on a regular basis.

By short, it is meant that the lender is agreeing to accept less than what is owed.

By refinance, it is meant that your original loan would be wiped out and a new loan put in place.

For example, you have a house that is worth $100,000., but the mortgage on the property is $150,000.

The new mortgage would be for about $90-94,000. And you would be starting over with a 30 year fixed rate.

There are two short refinance systems currently in use. The first, recently enacted with funding of some 50 *billion,* (with a B) will actually affect about 23 households in the United States. The first qualification for the program, is that the homeowner NOT be late or behind in their payments which leaves almost everyone out that is reading this book. The second reason is that the *lender* must be *willing* to start accepting less than what they have previously been receiving.

As I mentioned before, banks are only in it for the money. In short, *almost* NO lender will adjust the payments accepted downward while the homeowner is *current* and *up to date* on their payments.

Why should they? If you sold someone a boat for $1,000. and they were agreed to pay you $100 per month for ten months, isn't that what you would expect? If they came to you after 3 months and said, "This boat is only worth $500 now so please, let me just make 2 more payments and we'll call it even," would you do it? The key to this plan is that the banks must be WILLING to accept less than what was previously agreed. They usually are not. That is why I predict this wonderful government plan to help the homeowner may end up actually helping about 23 households. Do you wonder what the banks will do with the other 49 billion left over?

In the other type of short refinance, it's true that this is *also voluntary* from the bank, but the lender is a lot more likely to agree to accept less. Why? Motivation. When it looks like the only alternative is foreclosure and the homeowner actually IS behind in the payments, the high cost of foreclosing and actually having to take possession of a house is scary to them.

In both types of short refinance the lenders figuratively burn your old mortgage, wiping it totally off their books and a new, lower mortgage takes the place of the old.

There are several advantages to both you and the lender with this arrangement.

The lender will not have to foreclose and take possession of the property.

You will be able to stay in the home you've been living in and not have to move.

The lender will not run the risk of vandalism or destruction while it sits vacant.

Your payments will be lower and you'll have the knowledge that they won't "adjust" to ridiculous rates.

The lender will benefit if you should decide to sell at a later date.

The lender will have a higher mortgage on the property than if they "dumped it" in a foreclosure.

A short refinance is usually set up so that IF you should decide to sell in the future, the lender will then be owed the difference between what you owed originally and what the new mortgage amount was. (In other words, you can't owe 150,000 on the original mortgage, get a short refinance for $95,000, then turn around and sell the property a year later for $110,000 and pocket $15,000.)

Depending on how soon you sell after the short refinance, the lender will have a stake in the property so that IF you later sold for $110,000. The lender would receive all the proceeds but your credit would not be hurt in any way. (As long as you were current on your payment at the time of sale.)

In addition to the stipulation about selling the home after a short refinance, there is also the qualification factor.

As an example, let's say you bought a house for $150,000 and the payments each month including principle, interest, taxes and insurance (PITI) came to about $1300.

Now suppose something happens like a divorce, a job loss, a hospitalization or any other reason that keeps you from making that same payment of $1300. per month.

After missing 2 or more payments, the lender knows you are likely headed for foreclosure and MAY consider a short refinance.

Now your situation has changed and you can no longer afford the 1300 per month but you CAN afford say, $800 per month. If your home has dropped in value and is now worth around $100,000, then your PITI payment would be about $800 per month and the bank MAY consider the short refinance solution.

IF the lender will consider a short refinance, they will request several papers from you to evaluate your financial situation.

These papers will include last 2 years' tax return (with w-2's), last 2 months bank statements, last two paystubs, a hardship letter signed and dated, and a financial statement showing what your total income is compared to your total outgo.

The lender then sends out a real estate agent or broker to do what is called a Broker Price Opinion. (BPO)

A REAL appraisal of residential property from a *certified* appraiser usually costs anywhere between $300-600.

The lender gets the agent to do a "quickie" inspection or sometimes just a "drive by" for $40-50.

This tells the lender that the property is still there, it is occupied, (lenders will not do a short refinance on property that isn't occupied by the owner) and a ballpark estimate of resale value of the home.

A normal or average short refinance will usually take about 4-6 weeks.

Some lenders, such as Countrywide, (Now Bank of America) with more foreclosures than any other company in the nation, will not even consider a short refinance.

There are people (like myself) that will see if you are qualified for a short refinance and check with your lender to see if they would even consider this rare option.

Almost always, hiring a person to do the short refinance for you is a lot easier than trying to do it yourself.

Never, never pay anyone that is not an attorney any kind of upfront fee for any reason or promise of what they will do concerning "helping" you out of the foreclosure situation.

A typical fee for successfully getting a short refinance done for you by someone else is about $1500 paid ONLY if the short refinance is successful and ONLY at the time the papers for the new loan are signed.

The short refinance person qualifies you, checks with the lender on the possibility of the new lower loan, gets all the needed paperwork together, sends it to the lender, makes all the follow up phone calls, negotiates with the lender on your behalf, meets with the BPO person to get the new loan as low as possible for you, and checks over all the paperwork. These are the reasons why it will be a lot easier for you if you hire an experienced person to do all this for you. If you do it yourself and are unsuccessful, you've spent a lot of wasted time and effort. If you hire someone else and they are not successful, it hasn't cost you any time money or effort. If they ARE successful, the nominal fee charged will more than be made up in just 2-3 months with your lower payment schedule.

The average short refinance may save you anywhere between $200- $1800 per month.

Something you may have noticed is that it always seems to happen that whenever someone has misfortune, like possibly losing a house by means of a hurricane, death or divorce, there will be greedy, heartless persons trying to take advantage of the misfortune of others.

After hurricanes, people rush in with tap water in jugs, selling it for $5.00 a gallon, and when someone gets behind on their payments, these same people figure that since you aren't making the mortgage payment, there might be some extra money they could take off your hands.

If the person you are dealing with is not an Attorney or does not have either a real estate license or a mortgage broker license or even a business license, you are taking a tremendous risk. (Even though you may feel you have nothing left to lose.)

With the exception of you coming into a bundle of money and making up all the back payments, late fees, and Attorney costs, the next best thing the lender would like to work out with you is the...

The Loan Modification

Chapter Six

The main reason the banks love a loan modification (or loan mod) is for the simple reason that they are still getting *all* the money owed to them no matter what your home is worth.

A loan modification is only changing the terms of the loan – NOT the *amount* of the loan as it does in a short refinance.

For example, you have a loan amount of $150k on your house and the house is currently worth only $100k.

The lender takes all the back payments you have missed, puts it on the back end of the loan, changes your loan to a fixed rate and *maybe* drops the interest rate a small per-centage.

The result is now you owe MORE than $150K on your house, your new monthly payment is slightly more or slightly less than it was previously, (when you were unable to pay) and the lender is expecting you to "contribute" a one time, one month "good faith" payment which is NOT applied to ANY part of the mortgage note or any of the bank fees.

At the same time this is happening, houses in your subdivision similar to yours are *renting* for about ¾ to ½ (or less) than what your new current monthly payment is.

The way to qualify for the loan modification is to have had a *temporary* loss of income.

For example, you lost your job and were out of work for three or four months and you were unable to keep up the payments, but now you're employed again and making the same amount as before or maybe even a little more.

Possibly, you were hurt on the job or were in a car accident...*anything* that kept you from working and earning *temporarily,* but now your situation is back to normal.

A loan modification can take anywhere between 4 weeks to 4 months and the lender "promises" to repair the damage to your credit *if* you agree to the loan modification.

Some lenders are downright silly in their demands. They will take three months to decide they need another scrap of paper from you and then tell you that you have to get it back to them in 72 hours or they will go ahead and close the case.

As always, there are people willing to do all the legwork for you to get you a loan modification for a fee.

You have to count the cost of getting all the paperwork together, sitting on hold on the phone for hours, negotiating with the bank and then maybe being turned down anyway.

Never, pay anyone upfront to "try" to work a loan modification for you. Once these loan modification scammers have your money, absolutely nothing further will be done to help you.

The legitimate loan modification people will charge you about $1500 for the loan mod and this is *in addition* to the "contribution" the bank asks for. This is to be paid at the same time the "contribution" is contributed.

Always (if you aren't doing it yourself) agree to pay the loan modification fee only IF the people are successful in getting you the modified loan *on terms acceptable* to you.

There are people out there with a "loan modification business" that have never, ever actually *done* a loan modification, been a mortgage broker or been involved in real estate and finance in *any* way. Some of these people have listened to, or paid some "guru" at a seminar, "How to make a fortune in the pre-foreclosure business without a license."

So with no experience and no license, people are approaching you to let them "help you" out of your situation. Frankly, since these "real estate gurus" make their money off a national base of people that want to get rich quick, they sometimes advise their "students" to do things which are either illegal, unlawful, or unethical in the state where the student lives.

There are also people that *are* legitimate and work full time with the lenders all the time doing short refinances, loan modifications, short sales, etc.

A normal fee for a loan modification varies between $1200 -$1800, depending on the size of the loan and the service person or company getting the loan modification for you.

If you are able to qualify for a loan modification, there are some important questions to ask yourself about your home and your credit.

What is the difference between what you owe and what your house is worth? How long will it be before the market says your house is worth *more* than what you owe?

What is the difference between what your monthly payment is and what you could rent something comparable for?

If the loan modification doesn't go through, how much damage has already been done to your credit?

How much is your credit worth to you?

How long will your credit be affected by the situation you're currently facing?

If you could rent a similar house for $600-1800 less per month, could you use the difference to pay off other debts and help get your credit straightened out?

After answering these questions, it may be the time to consider...

Bankruptcy

Chapter Seven

There are 3 "chapters" concerning bankruptcy law, 7, 11, and 13.

A Chapter 7 bankruptcy is known as a liquidation of assets because just about anything you have of value will be sold, the monies collected, and the lenders paid at least something.

If you have an automobile you are making payments on, you can usually keep the car – as long as you keep making the payments.

If you are making the payments on your house, (your primary residence) you will be allowed to keep your house *if* you continue to make the regular monthly payments on it.

If you do not pay on either the house or the car, they *will* be repossessed, bankruptcy or no bankruptcy.

The main thing to consider is that Chapter 7 bankruptcy *does not* stop foreclosure –it only delays it for a while.

A chapter 13 bankruptcy *may* help you stop the foreclosure but, as usual, there are requirements.

A chapter 13 bankruptcy is a restructuring of debt and the minimum qualification is a steady income. If you are desperate to keep your house and other things like a car or boat or airplane even, it's possible to get your debt restructured.

When your debt is restructured, you must present a budget to the court and they will determine what you can afford to pay. Normally, the court will take all the money that you are behind in payments, add in the late fees and attorney costs and arrive at a lump sum called your arrearages.

Thirty to forty five days after Chapter 13 is filed, you will normally be required to resume *all* of your time payment obligations, but usually this is at a lower interest rate.

Next, your arrearages total is taken and divided by the number of months the court has given you to "get your act together". (60 months is the maximum amount of time allowed to get 100% caught up.)

So, for example, if your arrearages totaled $7,200, Then you would be required to pay an additional $120 per month on the arrearages. The main benefit of this option is, if you love your house and can't or don't want to move, you are allowed to stay in your house for as long as you comply with the court ordered plan.

If the chapter 13 is granted, the people that lent you the money have NO SAY on how much you are paying back each month on your arrearages, (at 0% interest!) *and* they may have to take a lower interest rate on your normal time payments.

Remember your regular monthly payments will continue at possibly reduced interest, and your arrearages are separate and at 0% interest. Sometimes, the attorney you hired to file the chapter 13, will also accept payments from you on a monthly basis.

Your creditors are required by law to accept your payments, and if you stay good on the payments for the entire five years (or whatever term the judge has decided) you are 100% discharged from all arrearages.

After 4-5 years on this plan, the only payments that should be left are the house payments and the usual things that recur forever – taxes, power, water, phones, food, clothing, etc.

One other benefit – if you file chapter 13 Bankruptcy even as little as one day before the foreclosure sale, the foreclosure sale is stopped.

The main problems with the chapter 13 are that 1.) You will be paying the same or more than what you were paying *before* you fell behind in your payments. 2.) Five years is a long time to go with no interruption of income, no medical problems, no layoffs, etc, and the ton of other stuff that happens to good people.

Like a loan modification, Chapter 13 is usually only granted when there has been a temporary loss of income.

For example, you've been working for a company and then you have an accident or get laid off for 3 months.

Three months later, you're back at work for the same or a different company making the same or more than you did previously. This kind of situation is ideal for the loan modification or the Chapter 13 bankruptcy.

It all sounds great but, you may still have the same problem as those that get a loan modification – you may still owe twice what you're house is worth.

A Chapter 11 bankruptcy is very similar to a Chapter 13. The difference is that Chapter 13 is set up mostly for individuals, while Chapter 11 is generally set up for corporations and partnerships.

It is estimated that *less* than 10% of *individuals* filing Chapter 11 are successful.

There have been major changes to the bankruptcy laws in the last few years and in the past, it was almost automatic that if you filed, a judge would declare you bankrupt.

Currently, *less* than 50% of all bankruptcies are successful and the days of do-it-yourself or getting a para-legal firm are fast disappearing.

If you talk to a bankruptcy attorney, there is a pretty good chance you'll get a recommendation to file for bankruptcy.

Surgeons recommend surgery, politicians recommend you vote for them, bakers recommend baked goods and life insurance salesman recommend life insurance.

This is our free enterprise system and I'm just saying that anything anyone recommends to you *may* be best for you, and it *may not.*

In addition to that, the person may be recommending the right thing for you and *still* not be the right person for you to get the product or service from.

However, a bankruptcy attorney will be most likely to guide you to the bankruptcy plan that is most likely to be successful for you.

Talk to an accountant about your situation. Bankruptcy may or may not be best for you in your situation and you don't want to pay $1500 upfront for an attorney that may or may not be successful. Some attorneys will waive (or partially waive) the fee if they are unsuccessful. Ask. It never hurts to ask. This applies to almost everything.

While you are in the *process* of foreclosure (from the time you file until the judge makes his decision) the lender(s) are prevented by law from doing anything that is considered a collection activity. (Like a shortsale.)

It is usually a few weeks to a month or two *after* the Judges' decision that the house will be foreclosed.

If you're planning a short sale, (more on this later) this can *sometimes* be done by excluding the house from the bankruptcy, but it isn't easy. Many people do a successful short sale *first* and *then* file for bankruptcy.

In addition to possibly getting rid of all your other debts, bankruptcy will prohibit the lender from filing what is known as a deficiency judgement. (If the house was included in the list of debts)

A deficiency judgement happens 100% of the time IF the house goes through foreclosure and wasn't listed on the list of debts in a successful bankruptcy. This also happens if the lender cannot sell the property for more than what is owed including late fees, back payments, and Attorney fees. What is owed on the home minus what is received for the home at foreclosure sale or auction is the *difference* or *deficiency.*

In a shortsale, the lender agrees to NOT file a deficiency judgement.

Whether you file for bankruptcy or just don't see the point in continuing to pay way more than you can rent a similar house for, the next best option after a short refinance or bankruptcy may be a ...

Short Sale

Chapter Eight

A few years ago, the words "Short sale" were rarely heard or used at all by the public and even some Real Estate agents had never even heard the term.

Basically, the term is taken from the lender being "shorted" or getting less than what is owed on the property in a payoff with the property being sold.

Many times I'm asked, "Why in the world would a lender that is owed $200k on a property agree to accept only $100k? I know it's the first question *I* asked the first time *I* ever heard the term.)

There is only one reason why lending institutions do anything at all and that is money. After all, money is their business and their *only* business.

If a lender has to foreclose, it typically costs between $30-$40k JUST to foreclose and that doesn't take into account the additional loss when the drop in property value is considered.

When a lender forecloses, it can take a year or more (depending on how much the homeowner is able to stall the process) and then a few more months while the home sits before it is finally sold.

All this time, the bank is not collecting any money and they are paying out for attorney fees, lawn service, electric, water and sometimes homeowners fees.

When the property sells, the lender has to pay Realtor fees, closing costs, and title insurance and they've been liable for any damages or lawsuits filed against the property while it is in their possession.

A short sale is a good solution for them as they will lose *less* money than they ordinarily would by foreclosing and they have the added advantage of *not* actually *owning* or having *possession* of your house.

It is possible to do a short sale yourself but, since the lender still will not let you receive any money from the sale, why would you do all the work, learn what you need to know, and spend your time for nothing in return?

You could always have an attorney do it but an attorney will charge an upfront fee and doesn't usually work with buyers of residential properties. Plus there is no guarantee of success.

The solution is a Realtor that knows what they are doing. It costs you nothing, takes only about 1 hour of your time getting the needed papers together and the Realtor does all the rest. This prevents foreclosure going on your record and if you have very little or no assets, the lender will not come after you for the difference.

The lender doesn't normally actually make a statement to the effect that they won't come after the homeowner, but they usually state something along the lines of, "Account settled. Not for full amount."

Anywhere in the phraseology where it says the account is settled it almost always means they're done. No pursuing, no collection activity, no future judgments or liens.

Even for a short sale, there are some qualifications the homeowner must meet for the lender to agree.

First and foremost, a homeowner must not be able to make the payment. Some people that are tremendously upside down on their house are able to make the payment but choose not to. Sometimes it's because they can rent an identical house for half what they pay on the monthly mortgage. Sometimes it's because they have recently *bought* an almost identical house for about half their previous mortgage. Sometimes they stop just ...because. The thinking may be, if the lender can't meet their obligations without a government subsidy (paid with YOUR tax dollars) why should you keep paying on a loan the lender KNEW you wouldn't be able to afford a few years down the road when the interest and payments adjusted upward?

Second, the homeowner must not have the equivalent of 4 or more mortgage payments in ALL checking and savings accounts. If you HAVE the money to pay but choose not to, don't try to hide your money in a FDIC bank. The lender *will* find it. (I recommend paying when you have the means to do so.)

Third, the homeowner must not have extensive assets that could easily be converted to cash to make the mortgage payments. (Like a boat, an airplane, or other property that is owned free and clear)

This qualification process is to weed out homeowners that are upside down on their house and just want out from under paying more than the house is worth for several years.

If you probably qualify for a short sale, the best thing to do is to get a real estate agent that knows what they are doing when it comes to short sales.

There is much more work involved and a large number of short sales fall through due to inexperienced and/or uneducated real estate agents.

If you are able to, ask around and don't take an agents word for how many short sales they have done.

The agent you are looking for will be able to *show* you (through copies of the sold section of the MLS) that they have successfully sold *and* closed at *least 12* short sales in the past 36 months.

Being the agent for the buyers in a shortsale doesn't count. It is actually more important that the agent was on the listing end of the short sale rather than the selling end as it is the listing agent that does all the short sale work involved.

Frankly, the toughest part of the buying agent job is to figuratively hold the buyers hand and reassure them that *eventually, probably,* they will get the house they want, regardless of how long the process is taking or how many delays come up.

To get a buyer for your home, the house must be able to be shown by other agents. Showing the home can be very complicated if there are renters in the property.

Renters often won't let the house be shown, they often do not pay rent, and sometimes they get an attorney that can keep them in the house until the day it is foreclosed.

The renters usually find out that the landlord (you) have not been making the payments because they are also served the same papers you are served to let them know what is going on and that the property is headed for foreclosure.

In my area, (Lake County) the process server that gives tenants the papers almost always advises them to NOT make any more rent payments.

It's true the process server likely feels bad for the tenants that are put in this situation. The tenants *do* need to save money because they *will* need to move out. However, the process server is giving legal advice when they tell the tenants this and could be in serious trouble for it. On the other hand, when the tenants ask the process server what they should do and he tells them to seek the advice of an attorney they may just do that and like I just mentioned, just about any real estate attorney could keep the tenants in the house rent free till after it's foreclosed.

Since the home will be sold as-is (you aren't going to make or pay for any repairs to be done) there is no reason to try to hide any defects that are on the property.

No matter how high or low the offer is, your net gain financially will always be zero, so if $5,000 or $500,000 is the difference between what is owed and what the property sells for, the net to you is still zero.

In the past, the I.R.S. would come after you for the difference between what you owed and what the home sold for as fully taxable income. (under the forgiven debt rule) The good news is that most people in foreclosure no longer have to worry about more taxes in addition to other money challenges.

In December of 2007, President Bush signed a new bill preventing the I.R.S. from collecting on the forgiven debt of the homeowner IF the home was the primary residence and the homeowner had lived in the home for 2 out of the past 5 years.

It's true that this law expires at the end of the 2009 tax year but there are a couple of different things that could happen.

President Obama may either extend the current law or sign a new one similar in it's place. (maybe one that is in effect permanently. It's absurd to demand a person that has lost his primary residence pay our government for that privilege) The only exception that I can think of is someone that walks away with cash after refinancing to the hilt and leaving the bank holding the bag.

If a person is termed insolvent, it simply means all their liabilities are greater than all their assets. Some banks about t be shut down are currently this way. If you are termed insolvent by the IRS, you are normally exempt from the debt forgiveness tax anyway.

More often than not, if a foreclosure sale is scheduled and a home is "in review" for a short sale, the lender will cancel or postpone the foreclosure sale.

Unfortunately, the sale is not canceled or postponed until within 72 hours of the sale taking place which unnerves most people including me. Numerous times the cancellation of foreclosure notice isn't faxed to the court until the day before foreclosure. (That's just from my own experience.)

Some lenders have actually misspoke (lied) and *said* the sale was cancelled and then foreclosure actually took place. (That has *also* been my experience)

One other requirement that I neglected to mention earlier because it only affects the homeowner indirectly, is that in a short sale, *the purchaser* of the home may NOT be related (a relative) of the person that currently owns the home in default. This is to prevent a relative from buying the home at a lower than market price and then deeding it back to the current homeowner. This is an example of the homeowner benefitting *indirectly* which is prohibited.

The final option available to you that is in some ways worse than doing absolutely nothing is called...

Deed-in-lieu-of-foreclosure

Chapter Nine

Of all the different options, this is by far the best one for the lender and the worst for you. (That is, unless you have already moved out or it's an investment property.)

If there is more than one mortgage on the property, or if there are other liens against the property, the lender is usually unable to do the deed-in-lieu.

One possible benefit to you in this option is that IF the lender is ready, willing, and able to do it, they USUALLY do not come after you for the difference.

The only other possible benefit to a deed-in-lieu of foreclosure for you is what is called the cash for keys program.

To be eligible for the cash for keys program, you must still be living in the house when the foreclosure process has legally started.

You must also leave the home in clean condition, free of any debris, and no unwanted items left behind.

In addition to the above requirements, you will be expected to list the home with a real estate agent for a minimum of ninety days. If the house doesn't sell during that time, then at least the bank knows what the house WON'T sell for and it's possible they will change their mind (*they* say "rescind their offer") and NOT do a deed-in-lieu.

During this listing period, the bank will expect you to actually try to sell the house – even if it is on a short sale basis.

Don't worry about paying a commission or closing costs or actually anything at all if the house should sell. This works exactly the same as the short sale mentioned earlier in this book because that is exactly what it is. If after ninety days of not even having an offer on the property, the bank may or may not offer you the deed-in-lieu option.

In a market like the one we are currently experiencing in Florida, many lenders are simply not offering the deed-in-lieu option because they already have too many homes on their books.

In Appendix A – How banks work, you'll find out more about the strange paradox that as long as you still have the house, the bank considers it an asset even if you are not paying. If they take possession of the house, they consider it at that time a liability!

If the lender actually has to take possession of your house, your house will go on their REO list. REO stands for Real Estate Owned.

If you have tenants in your house and you live elsewhere, THEY may be the ones that are offered the cash for keys deal to move out. This will be to your advantage since the tenants aren't going to pay rent anymore and they can make it impossible to show the house while they are still living in it. The bank will want to put their own lock and lockbox on the front door so it's important to have your Realtor be in touch with them

If it's you or the tenants, the lender will not pay any money until either has moved out and the house is vacant, left in the condition I described earlier.

Here's a tip. If you are offered this program, you don't have to paint, shampoo carpets, or do any repairs to make the house "perfect."

As far as your credit goes, most lenders will not tell you that a deed-in-lieu will affect your credit every bit as much as a regular foreclosure... but it does.

Sometimes, the lender will even not be honest (lie) when asked by the homeowner if it is better for their credit to do a deed-in-lieu rather than a foreclosure. It's not.

The only benefit to you if your lender is willing to do the deed-in-lieu is that they aren't *supposed* to file for a deficiency judgement.

Some lenders will ask you to sign a statement that you agree and understand that they (the lender) are NOT waiving their rights to come after you for the difference.

This usually happens if they suspect that you are hiding some assets that you didn't mention when you filled out your financial statement. It also happens if you own another residence.

An additional negative with the deed-in-lieu is that you absolutely will be moving out much sooner than if you choose any other option.

The lis pendens states that you MUST respond within 20 days and *some people believe* this means they must be moved out within that 20 days or the house will be foreclosed and they'll be thrown out. Not true.

However, you should respond to the lis pendens by writing to the judge assigned to your case. The name of the Judge will be in the court records.

By responding without an attorney, this is known as a "pro se" response and it is perfectly acceptable to respond without an attorney if you aren't going to employ one. If you are going to use an attorney, do NOT do this response yourself.

Do not waste your time answering to the attorney that filed on your lenders behalf, *that* attorney is NOT on your side and *that* attorney is NOT looking out for your best interest.

Just about everything you need to know to make an informed choice has been revealed. For the many readers that just want to know the bottom line, the last chapter is...

Summing Up

Chapter 10

There are many options available to you, the homeowner, in the foreclosure situation.

Not all options actually stop foreclosure and any person or group that tells you that they can <u>stop</u> (not delay) foreclosure, you can continue to live in the house, and you won't have to make any more mortgage payments is, pure and simple, lying to you.

Let's go over the options available:

Doing nothing – Unfortunately, the number one choice when people know they are unable to make up the back payments and do not realize they have legal rights and options.

The advantages of doing nothing are – well, if you do nothing at all, you'll know you stayed in the house as long as you could *without delaying* the foreclosure process *or* asserting your rights.

The disadvantages are that,

1.) The foreclosure process goes much faster,

2.) You'll be out much sooner,

3.) Your lender will win by default because that's what happens when you don't exercise your judicial rights.

4.) The home is still foreclosed,

5.) Your credit is shot for the next several years,

6.) A deficiency is *always* filed and

7.) The lender may come after you for the difference (the deficiency) for the next 20 years. (Renewing the 10 year judgment for another ten years.)

Stretchers – These are the homeowners that use all the rights, choices and options available to them to *stretch out* the length of time before the home is actually foreclosed, but, the home is still foreclosed, a deficiency is filed, and the lender may come after you for the next 20 years. (See above.) Just slightly different than the doing nothing options.

Beware of individuals that are not attorneys that will offer to keep you in the home as long as possible and just charge you a small monthly fee ($100-$500) to "keep" you in your home as long as possible. It's a scam. Some do nothing at all except collect their monthly fee for 3 or 4 months.

The advantages are,
1.) You will be staying in your home for the longest possible time,
2.) You aren't paying any mortgage payments,
3.) You are exercising all the rights and strategies at your disposal that you are entitled to by law.

The disadvantages are,
1.) Unless you do a short sale, the house still eventually forecloses and that is put on your permanent credit record and there *will* be a deficiency judgement
2.) Unless you hire someone that knows the ins and outs of exercising all the rights you're entitled to, you're likely to be out long before you needed to be,
3.) Attorneys don't work for free and they don't guarantee results or your money back.

Deed-in-lieu – IF the lender is willing to accept this option, (fewer and fewer are in this economy) the homeowner gives up the home in the shortest possible time. (Aside from moving out immediately.)

The only advantage to the homeowner is that by accepting the deed, the lender will *sometimes* agree to not pursue further collection activity with you.

Bankruptcy – This will delay the foreclosure activity while you are in the process but in the end, the property will still be foreclosed. (unless you are able to do a chapter 13 bankruptcy)

Disadvantage to bankruptcy is,
1.) The cost, (usually paid upfront)
2.) The effect on your credit, (usually for the next 7-10 years)
3.) The possibility the bankruptcy is unsuccessful, (more than 50% are!) and
4.) The house is still foreclosed.

Plus, in a chapter 13 bankruptcy, you may still owe far more than the property is worth and you will be on an extremely tight budget for the next few years. If something should happen during the reconstructive process, another restructuring option will _not_ be available.

The advantage to bankruptcy (if it is successful) is,
1.) _All_ your listed debts are wiped out, (with the exception of cars, boats, planes, or houses) and
2.) The lenders are not permitted further collection activity.

Plus, in chapter 13 bankruptcy, you can stay in your house and it doesn't get foreclosed.

Loan modification – the same people that helped put you into that ridiculous adjustable or variable rate mortgage that they _knew_ you wouldn't have qualified for once the rates adjusted, MAY be willing to let you keep on paying them on a lower interest, fixed rate mortgage.

The advantages are that
1.)You keep your house, (unless you default on the payments again)
2.) The lender has the lawsuit dismissed without prejudice, and
3.) Every payment made after the loan modification is done will help toward restoring your credit.

The disadvantages are that, in this market,
1.) You may still be paying almost twice what the same house in the same neighborhood would rent for.
2.) You will still be paying at, near, or more than what your previous payments were.
3.) Sometimes the lender will lead you to believe they are going to do a loan mod and _they are still actively pursuing_ the foreclosure. (Sometimes, they know immediately whether you will qualify or not qualify and yet, do not reveal this to you)

Short Refinance – Imagine selling your home at the current market value (whatever it is) and the new buyer has a new, 30 year fixed rate with mortgage payments about half of what you were paying. Now imagine that YOU are the new buyer of your own home. That is what a Short refinance is in simple terms.

The advantages of a short refinance are,
1.) You get to stay in your home
2.) You no longer owe more than the home is worth
3.)If you qualify for the short refinance, the new payments are something you can afford
4.) The new loan is a fixed rate,
5.) Each on time monthly payment helps restore your credit.

The disadvantages of a short refinance are,
1.) You must fit in to a very narrow range of homeowners (it's not based on credit)
2.) Very few lenders are doing this program,
3.) If you try to sell your home in the near future, the lender wants at least 50% of the difference between the old loan and the new loan,
4.) Because of # 3, very few owners would gain enough equity in the next ten years to walk away from the closing table with any money in their pocket.

The Short Sale – Actually having your lender agree to accept less than what is owed to them.

The advantages are,
1.) All the advantages of a _stretcher_,
2.) The home does _not_ go into foreclosure,
3.) The lender does NOT come after you for the difference,
4.) It doesn't cost you a dime,
5.) Unlike the stretchers on their own, your Realtor (if they know what they are doing) will take care of all the dealings with your lender to let you have the best of all the available options.

The disadvantages are,
1.) The occasional inconvenience of letting your home be shown to prospective, qualified buyers,
2.) Only having about 30 days from the time your lender gives _written_ acceptance of an offer to move out. (You will have 15-30 days before this period to know whether your lender is _probably_ going to accept or reject since the loss mitigator has to submit an approved acceptance for someone higher up to approve it also and written acceptance usually comes 5-10 days after verbal acceptance)

Let's take a final look at the different options and the final results.

Pay up ...all back payments, attorney fees, and late fees. No foreclosure, but also *not* likely to happen.

Doing nothing ... Ends in foreclosure.

Short refinance ...owe what house is currently worth and *no foreclosure*. Tough to qualify.

Loan modification...probably owe way more than the house is worth plus much higher payments than rent but *no foreclosure*. Only 1 in 4 qualify.

Bankruptcy ...Chapter 11, unlikely for non-corporate entities. Chapter 13, *no foreclosure* but tough to qualify for and real tight budget for next five years. Chapter 7, wipes out debts but house still gets *foreclosed*.

Short Sale ...no cost, *no foreclosure*, can stay in home rent free while the *minimum* 90 day process takes place.

Deed—in-lieu ...no cost, *no foreclosure* IF the house sells during the required 90 day listing period on a shortsale basis. *If* not short sold and *if* the bank is agreeable, they *may* accept the deed. No matter what the bank tells you, your credit is hurt *equally* with a *foreclosure* as it is with a deed-in-lieu.

Stretcher ...This takes a lot of specialized knowledge and an attorney will cost you money to do this option which will still *end in foreclosure.* A competent Realtor can keep you in the home for quite a while at no cost to you and then *prevent foreclosure with a short sale.*

What now? – Frankly, only you can decide this. It is *your* house, *your* credit, *your* life and everyone has a different situation.

What are *your* goals, objectives, desires?
In other words, after looking realistically at the different options and choices available, *What would you like to see happen in this situation? Is it possible? Is it probable?*

What are the resources available to you? Friends? Family? A Realtor? An Attorney? (*Not* the lenders attorney) Assets? Knowledge? ... What is the *best thing* for *you* in *your* situation? *That* is what you should do.

If you live in Lake County, you have one more resource, me. I'll discuss your unique situation with you, look in depth at the options, talk about how much time each process will take, and see if together, we can plan a course of action for you. There is no obligation.

If you don't live in Lake County, you have one more resource, me. No matter where you live outside Lake County, but still in the state of Florida, I have a network of experienced Realtors that can talk with you personally about your situation to help plan a course of action with no obligation also.

If you can send me an e-mail, leave your name, address of the property, and a brief description of your situation and you will receive a reply within 72 hours.

My e-mail address is: avoidfloridaforeclosure@gmail.com

Thank you for showing enough concern about your situation to find out what options are available to you.

APPENDIX A

How Banks Really Work
or

Why you shouldn't feel guilty about staying in your home as long as you legally can.

If you scare easily when it comes to the economy, it might be best for you to skip this whole appendix.

If I asked you to show me some money, most of you would hold up some paper cash. This cash is *not* money. Look at the bill you are holding. It says, "Federal Reserve *Note*"

What is a note? A note is a promise to pay. At closing, you signed a mortgage and a note. The note was your promise to pay and the mortgage was the security to back up the promise. Take your Federal Reserve Note to a bank teller and tell them, "I would like to exchange this note backed by the Federal Reserve for money." The teller will tell you, "That IS money."

If it IS money, why does it say "NOTE"? If a note is a promise to pay, (and it is) what is the Federal Reserve promising to pay? ... More notes. More promises to pay.

When people started waking up to this fact, the federal reserve added some words that now meant that even though it was a note (a promise to pay) it was to be considered as money just because they say it is.

"This **note** is legal tender (money) for all debts public and private." What a deal. Need to pay bills? Just print up some more paper, call it money, and arrest anyone else that does it. That's the Federal Reserve at work.

What is a dollar? A "dollarweight" from which we get the term dollar, is 1/20 of an ounce. Back in the day, a dollar was worth 1/20 of an ounce of GOLD. If you took 20 one dollar bills you could actually exchange them for an ounce of Gold. Now it takes between 30-40 TIMES that amount to get the same ounce of gold. This is inflation.

You know the rest, the price of gold went up due to inflation to around $35 an ounce and our government set it there as a *standard* and then made it illegal for Americans to buy Gold (coin or bullion) either here or overseas and bringing it back here.

While Nixon was President, he took us *off* the Gold Standard entirely and the price of gold immediately shot upward.

So what are the Federal Reserve Notes, these promises to pay backed by? Most bankers and politicians would say, "Faith in the strength and integrity of the United States Government."

Little problem here. The Federal Reserve, which prints up these green colored, paper promises to pay, is NOT a part of the United States Government. It's not a branch of our government, it isn't even a twig.

Did you ever wonder when you hear about "the National Debt" just who do (to whom for you English majors) we, as Americans, "owe" this money to?

Ourselves. A little more than half the debt is for government bonds and the like and the rest is for other government entities which is circular as, "We, the People" own all that our government owns from assets to liabilities.

More than 600 Billion (with a B) goes to pay *just the interest alone.* So our government cannot meet its obligations without "robbing Peter to pay Paul."

Are you ready for the next shocker?

There are two types of banking done in the world. "100% reserve banking" is one and the other is called "fractional reserve banking.

With 100% reserve banking, you go down to the bank, deposit $1,000 in a savings account, the bank pays you about ½ of 1% to you and then lends this $1,000 to someone else for 6 ½ %. (Or more) The bank operates on this 6% difference between what is brought IN to the bank by those that save and what goes OUT to the customers in the form of a loan.

This is not the way our banks here in America work. This is the actual system in most other places in the world. Banking is done by what is called fractional reserve banking.

With fractional banking (in the U.S.A.) the fraction is currently between 10-25 %. What that means is that you go down to the bank, deposit $1,000 in a savings account, the bank pays you about ½ to 1% to you and then is able to lend out **4 to10 TIMES the amount of** your deposit, or $10,000.

Let's look at the numbers. With 100% reserve banking, $1,000. deposited to a savings account would yield to the bank about $60. (6 ½ minus ½ = 6%) With the same $1,000 deposited with our fractional system, the bank lends out $10,000 and receives a return of about $600. (again, 6 ½ minus ½ = 6%)

Hold on! If only $1,000 is deposited in the bank and they get $600 (per year!) based on lending out 10 times the deposit, they really are getting a 60% return – on YOUR money. So in 2 years, there would be a 120% return, or *more* than your deposit *plus* the interest they paid you.

Is it any wonder that one of the major lending institutions that went under gave the CEO that RAN THE COMPANY INTO THE GROUND a severance and bonus package worth 72 MILLION for the previous year?

72 MILLION! By golly, there are professional athletes that have to "work" two ENTIRE seasons for that kind of money.

If the average person making $25,000 per year worked for 40 years, they would make 1 million over their lifetime, so 72 MILLION is what the "average" person would make in just 72 ...LIFETIMES!

With the fractional reserve system we have in use, no one is surprised that the bankers are making a fortune using the average persons money. Don't forget, they aren't using any of their *own* money, just the money that average people like you and me have deposited for them to use.

Maybe our government learned the trick from the banks about making the people think that they themselves actually have any money to help us. The truth is, the only money they have comes from the very people they are "helping". All money our government has is first collected from taxpayers.

This is why lenders do NOT want your house. They can make a ton *more* money *with* money than they can with real estate... especially real estate that has been going down in value for the last 2 1/2 years.

Lenders are not in the real estate business, they are in the money lending business and every time they have to take possession of a house, it represents money that is tied up and can't be lent out.

For example, if they take possession of a house that has a value of $100,000 dollars they are prohibited by law from lending out $400,000.

If they were charging just 6% on that $400k it would be a return of $24k or **$2,000 per month** that would be lost over the $100k house in their possession. What's worse, if the house sits for a year, the lender has lost the equivalent of 24% of the value (100k-24k) on the money they couldn't lend out!

That is why *when the bank owns your house* it is considered a liability *but when you own your house* it is considered an asset. This is also why even if a bank shows assets (promises to pay) that are *more* than their liabilities (actual cash and homes in their possession) they can be closed down. The assets must be *at least* 4 times the liabilities or they are in financial trouble.

Your house is considered an asset because of the PROMISE TO PAY. The NOTE is the mortgage. We promise to pay one note with some other notes.

The bank lends out money with the idea that the homeowner will fulfill the obligation or the promise to pay.

If everyone that had money in a checking account, savings account, CD's, etc. in a bank all came to clean out their accounts on the same day, you know what would happen.

The bank would close down. Why? The answer is because the bank would *not* be able to fulfill the obligations, or, promises to pay.

Ironically, *the bank is banking* on everyone they have lent *your money to,* to meeting and fulfilling their obligations to the bank, and AT THE SAME TIME they are also banking on *the bank itself* to NOT have to fulfill *their* promises or meet *their* obligations.

The bank expects everyone else to meet their obligations and liabilities and can succeed only if the bank itself doesn't have to meet its' own obligations and liabilities.

Think about it. If the bank took back every home that was mortgaged, they would have a slew of houses and very little money or NO money to lend. Do they make more money selling the houses or by lending out 4 times the money they get from selling houses?

That is why they are in the banking business and not the real estate business.

So without YOU, the hardworking tax payer, neither our government nor the banks would be able to meet their obligations.

APPENDIX B

9 Signs to Watch Out for When People Want to "Help" you

1.) No Need to talk to your bank.

A common warning sign of fraud is when any arrangements with you and the person are asked to be kept secret from your lender. They tell you that they will do all the talking and negotiating with the bank so that you won't need to. This tactic keeps the lender from telling you that the person "helping" you is, in fact, doing nothing at all. No body that wants business dealings kept private and "just between you and me" is doing things ethically. True, I *do* tell clients that they don't NEED to negotiate with the bank, but it doesn't matter to me if they talk with the lender or not.

2.) Thanks for your house, now get out!

In spite of what a scammer may have told you about living rent free. Some will give you an eviction notice within days of you signing your property over to them. If the person "helping" you has a record at the courthouse of filing for evictions, you just might be their next victim.

3.) I'll take your problem house off your hands.

The first thing the "Get Rich in Foreclosures" gurus often tell their eager listeners is to simply ask the homeowner to just give them the house. I've encountered homeowners that not only signed the house over to a total stranger but also gave them "power of attorney" concerning the house as well! When I asked them why they would do such a thing the homeowners told me that the person had sent them a postcard that "guaranteed" to solve all their house and loan problems while letting them live in the house rent free. The postcard came from a town in another county and had a P.O. box for a return address!

4.) The company I work for does this all the time.

Many con artists make it appear as though they are part of some huge organization with vast resources to "help" you. I've seen postcards with big office buildings on them implying this was where the business was and the person that sent the postcard worked. I met a homeowner that called on one of these postcards and the person coming out didn't even have their name on their business card! When questioned about it, the person said, "Oh, I don't bother with that because everyone knows me around here." You can almost hear the "ding, ding, ding" of the scam alert on that one. If someone that talks to you about helping is not an attorney, does not have either a Mortgage Brokers license or a Real Estate license, watch out! There is a reason why someone involved in financing or real estate does *not* have a license. They may be totally inexperienced, they may not have any knowledge (other than the "get rich quick gurus") and they may have *had* a license but it was taken away for unethical behavior. The person with a license MUST deal with you honestly, fairly, and ethically or they are in danger of losing their license and livelihood. A person without a license has nothing to lose except maybe freedom. That is, *if* they get caught, *if* they get prosecuted, and *if* they are convicted. One of these "get rich quick in real estate" gurus living here in Florida is *still* serving jail time for his lack of ethics. He must have known all about real estate and finances because he was a former busboy clearing tables!

5.) Stopping foreclosure scams.

Pure and simple, they don't work. There is no way you can continue to live in your home *and* **not** pay on a mortgage, short of paying the whole mortgage off.

There are only two ways to avoid foreclosure, stay in your home, and pay a mortgage that is more in line with current market value. One is the chapter 13, restructuring of debt, bankruptcy, (Though you may still owe more than your house is worth with this one.) the other is the short refinance. With a loan modification, you avoid foreclosure and stay in the house, but are paying about the same or more than you were before you were unable to make the payments. If your home is worth less than what you owe and you do not qualify for any of these other programs, the *short sale* is the only other way to actually stop foreclosure and, since it IS a sale, you must be leaving the home behind.

6.) Signing the papers.

Not letting you take time to read through the papers, or not wanting your lawyer to look at the papers is common. One of the "get rich quick foreclosure" gurus proved his point about people signing without reading by having all attendees at his last seminar sign a bunch of papers. More than 90% signed a paper that said, "I understand by signing this paper that I am releasing to the public absolute proof that I don't read things before signing them." A day or even a week is not that critical when it comes to the foreclosure process so take time to read everything. Sometimes just asking, "Do you mind if I take these papers to my Lawyer and make sure I'm doing the right thing?" will be sufficient to flush out a scammer. If they sort of agree but refuse to leave the papers with you, don't even let them back in the house after you kick them out. When I have homeowners sign a listing contract, not only are they free to have a lawyer check the papers out but I also tell them to NOT do a short sale if their attorney has a better plan and that there is absolutely no cost to them at any time for any reason. (Including withdrawal of the listing.)

7.) In a Company we trust?

A variation of the scammer having you sign over the deed to them personally is to have you sign over your deed to a trust, with a third party trustee. An example of how this works is, say you have a home worth that you owe $150,000 on and it's currently worth $100,000. You sign your house over to a trust and they negotiate with the bank to take the lowest price the bank can live with which is maybe $80,000. Meanwhile, they try to find a buyer for your property for $95,000. It all comes together for them if the bank accepts the $80k, and the buyer agrees to pay $95K. The "trust" literally pockets the $15,000 difference. With prices dropping like they have this past year, more and more scammers are finding it hard to find buyers willing to pay much more than what the trust has negotiated with the bank. If the deal doesn't work out for the trust, they just deed the property back to you right before foreclosure.

Signing the deed over to an individual or a trust where your underlying mortgage is *not* paid off means that YOU are still liable until that mortgage no longer exists.

8. The Old Standby.

Last on our list is one that applies to Real Estate and just about everything in the world. "If it sounds too good to be true, it probably IS too good to be true."   You owe $150K on your house. You know it might be worth possibly $145-$150. You get a letter in the mail that says something along the lines of, "My wife and I are interested in buying your home, we've always wanted to live in "X" (whatever town you live in) or "I'll give you $5k or $10k over your mortgage plus make up all your back payments and fees." Personally, I tend to fall for the "This ointment will put a full head of beautiful, luxuriant hair on your bald head" ads. Anything that tells you exactly what you want to hear is more than likely a lie at worst, and an exaggeration at best.

9.) I'm only here to help.

Ask anyone helping you why they are helping you. They should say how much money they expect to make, how they expect to make it, and who they expect to pay them. If they won't state this and say something vague like, I just want to help people, show them the door. No legitimate licensed person works for free. There are exceptions. A lawyer *may* do pro bono work and a Realtor or Mortgage broker *may* help out a really good friend or relative. In the case of a shortsale, the bank pays the Realtors' fees.

If the person you are dealing with is a total stranger, don't believe for one second, "They just like to help people and you were selected to be "helped" next."

APPENDIX C
YOUR FORECLOSURE RIGHTS

1.) The Right to Defend

You don't have to give up your house immediately just because the bank wants their house back. Florida is a judicial foreclosure state and all foreclosures are handled with proper legal procedure. The only way you lose your rights is to just pack up and leave. The banks have attorneys that handle these cases all day long and they just plain aren't used to anyone putting up any kind of fight and *any* resistance delays your case. The longer your case is delayed, the more likely you are to get your way concerning a loan mod, a short refinance or a short sale.

2.) The Right to Discovery

This enables you to request documents from the bank. The main thing to request is the *original note* (not a copy) signed by you in blue ink. Almost always when your note has been sold or reassigned, this note is lost. The lender must establish their right to even foreclose without this *original note.* You can also find out if the lender has violated some rule of foreclosure (which happens more often than you think)

3.) Right of Proof

The burden of proof is on the lender.
This means that the lender (not you) must gather all the evidence and prove every part of their case. The level of proof is just a preponderance of the evidence which is a lot easier than *beyond a reasonable doubt.* Preponderance simply means *more likely than not* but, sometimes, even this is enough to help you win your case.

4.) Right to Counterclaim

There are a multitude of laws governing lending practices and these laws are often changing. If you are in a home that you never should have been qualified to buy in the first place or if the lender used deceptive language or just plain made a mistake. Consult an attorney and have them take a good long look at your loan to see if you have a case (you always have a case) but more importantly, if you possibly have a winnable case.

APPENDIX D

Florida Foreclosure Law

702.01 Equity.

702.03 Certain foreclosures validated.

702.035 Legal notice concerning foreclosure proceedings.

702.04 Mortgaged lands in different counties.

702.05 Mortgaged lands sold for taxes.

702.06 Deficiency decree; common-law suit to recover deficiency.

702.065 Final judgment in uncontested proceedings where deficiency judgment waived; attorney's fees when default judgment entered.

702.07 Power of courts and judges to set aside foreclosure decrees at any time before sale.

702.08 Effect of setting aside foreclosure decree.

702.09 Definitions.

702.10 Order to show cause; entry of final judgment of foreclosure; payment during foreclosure.

702.01 Equity.--All mortgages shall be foreclosed in equity. In a mortgage foreclosure action, the court shall sever for separate trial all counterclaims against the foreclosing mortgagee. The foreclosure claim shall, if tried, be tried to the court without a jury.

History.--RS 1987; GS 2501; RGS 3844; CGL 5747; s. 7, ch. 22858, 1945; s. 2, ch. 87-217.

702.03 Certain foreclosures validated.--All mortgage foreclosures heretofore made, or now pending, wherein there has been annexed to the bill of complaint in such cause, an uncertified copy of the mortgage, as provided by chapter 12095, Acts of 1927, entitled: "An act to amend section 3845 RGS relating to complaint in foreclosure of mortgages" are hereby validated and confirmed insofar as they relate to the copy of the mortgage attached to such complaint, to the same extent and effect as if section 3117, RGS, had been expressly repealed by chapter 12095, 1927, entitled: "An act to amend section 3845 RGS relating to complaint in foreclosure of mortgages."

History.--s. 1, ch. 13642, 1929; CGL 1936 Supp. 5748(1).

702.035 Legal notice concerning foreclosure proceedings.--Whenever a legal advertisement, publication, or notice relating to a foreclosure proceeding is required to be placed in a newspaper, it is the responsibility of the petitioner or petitioner's attorney to place such advertisement, publication, or notice. For counties with more than 1 million total population as reflected in the 2000 Official Decennial Census of the United States Census Bureau as shown on the official website of the United States Census Bureau, any notice of publication required by this section shall be deemed to have been published in accordance with the law if the notice is published in a newspaper that has been entered as a periodical matter at a post office in the county in which the newspaper is published, is published a minimum of 5 days a week, exclusive of legal holidays, and has been in existence and published a minimum of 5 days a week, exclusive of legal holidays, for 1 year or is a direct successor to a newspaper that has been in existence for 1 year that has been published a minimum of 5 days a week, exclusive of legal holidays. The advertisement, publication, or notice shall be placed directly by the attorney for the petitioner, by the petitioner if acting pro se, or by the clerk of the court. Only the actual costs charged by the newspaper for the advertisement, publication, or notice may be charged as costs in the action.

History.--s. 4, ch. 2001-215; s. 7, ch. 2006-175; s. 2, ch. 2007-185.

702.04 Mortgaged lands in different counties.-- When a mortgage includes lands, railroad track, right-of-way, or terminal facilities and station grounds, lying in two or more counties, it may be foreclosed in any one of said counties, and all proceedings shall be had in that county as if all the mortgaged land, railroad track, right-of-way, or terminal facilities and station grounds lay therein, except that notice of the sale must be published in every county wherein any of the lands, railroad track, right-of-way, or terminal facilities and station grounds to be sold lie. After final disposition of the suit, the clerk of the circuit court shall prepare and forward a certified copy of the decree of foreclosure and sale and of the decree of confirmation of sale to the clerk of the circuit court of every county wherein any of the mortgaged lands, railroad tracks, right-of-way, or terminal facilities and station grounds lie, to be recorded in the foreign judgment book of each such county, and the costs of such copies and of the record thereof shall be taxed as costs in the cause.

History.--RS 1989; s. 1, ch. 4420, 1895; GS 2503; s. 1, ch. 7339, 1917; RGS 3846; CGL 5749.

702.05 Mortgaged lands sold for taxes.--Any person who has a lien by mortgage or otherwise upon lands sold for taxes may, within the time allowed by law for redemption, redeem such lands, and the receipt of the officer authorized to receive the amount paid for redemption money shall entitle the lienholder to collect the said amount, with interest at the rate of 10 percent per annum, as a part of and in the same manner as the amount secured by her or his original lien.

History.--s. 1, ch. 3903, 1889; RS 1990; GS 2504; RGS 3847; CGL 5750; s. 783, ch. 97-102.

702.06 Deficiency decree; common-law suit to recover deficiency.--In all suits for the foreclosure of mortgages heretofore or hereafter executed the entry of a deficiency decree for any portion of a deficiency, should one exist, shall be within the sound judicial discretion of the court, but the complainant shall also have the right to sue at common law to recover such deficiency, provided no suit at law to recover such deficiency shall be maintained against the original mortgagor in cases where the mortgage is for the purchase price of the property involved and where the original mortgagee becomes the purchaser thereof at foreclosure sale and also is granted a deficiency decree against the original mortgagor.

History.--s. 1, ch. 11993, 1927; CGL 5751; s. 1, ch. 13625, 1929.

702.065 Final judgment in uncontested proceedings where deficiency judgment waived; attorney's fees when default judgment entered.--

(1) In uncontested mortgage foreclosure proceedings in which the mortgagee waives the right to recoup any deficiency judgment, the court shall enter final judgment within 90 days from the date of the close of pleadings. For the purposes of this subsection, a mortgage foreclosure proceeding is uncontested if an answer not contesting the foreclosure has been filed or a default judgment has been entered by the court.

(2) In a mortgage foreclosure proceeding, when a default judgment has been entered against the mortgagor and the note or mortgage provides for the award of reasonable attorney's fees, it is not necessary for the court to hold a hearing or adjudge the requested attorney's fees to be reasonable if the fees do not exceed 3 percent of the principal amount owed at the time of filing the complaint, even if the note or mortgage does not specify the percentage of the original amount that would be paid as liquidated damages. Such fees constitute liquidated damages in any proceeding to enforce the note or mortgage. This section does not preclude a challenge to the reasonableness of the attorney's fees.

History.--s. 2, ch. 2001-215.

702.07 Power of courts and judges to set aside foreclosure decrees at any time before sale.--The circuit courts of this state, and the judges thereof at chambers, shall have jurisdiction, power, and authority to rescind, vacate, and set aside a decree of foreclosure of a mortgage of property at any time before the sale thereof has been actually made pursuant to the terms of such decree, and to dismiss the foreclosure proceeding upon the payment of all court costs.

History.--s. 1, ch. 11881, 1927; CGL 5752.

702.08 Effect of setting aside foreclosure decree.-- Whenever a decree of foreclosure has been so rescinded, vacated, and set aside and the foreclosure proceedings dismissed as provided in s. 702.07, the mortgage, together with its lien and the debt thereby secured, shall be, both in law and equity, completely relieved of all effects of any kind whatsoever resulting from or on account of the foreclosure proceedings and the decree of foreclosure and fully restored in all respects to the original status of the same as it existed prior to the foreclosure proceedings and the decree of foreclosure, and thereafter the same shall be for all purposes whatsoever legally of force and effect just as if foreclosure proceeding had never been instituted and a decree of foreclosure had never been made.

History.--s. 2, ch. 11881, 1927; CGL 5753.

702.09 Definitions.--For the purposes of ss. 702.07 and 702.08 the words "decree of foreclosure" shall include a judgment or order rendered or passed in the foreclosure proceedings in which the decree of foreclosure shall be rescinded, vacated, and set aside; the word "mortgage" shall mean any written instrument securing the payment of money or advances and includes liens to secure payment of assessments arising under chapters 718 and 719 and liens created pursuant to the recorded covenants of a homeowners' association as defined in s. 712.01; the word "debt" shall include promissory notes, bonds, and all other written obligations given for the payment of money; the words "foreclosure proceedings" shall embrace every action in the circuit or county courts of this state wherein it is sought to foreclose a mortgage and sell the property covered by the same; and the word "property" shall mean and include both real and personal property.

History.--s. 3, ch. 11881, 1927; CGL 5754; s. 4, ch. 2002-27; s. 13, ch. 2003-14.

702.10 Order to show cause; entry of final judgment of foreclosure; payment during foreclosure.--

(1) After a complaint in a foreclosure proceeding has been filed, the mortgagee may request an order to show cause for the entry of final judgment and the court shall immediately review the complaint. If, upon examination of the complaint, the court finds that the complaint is verified and alleges a cause of action to foreclose on real property, the court shall promptly

issue an order directed to the defendant to show cause why a final judgment of foreclosure should not be entered.

(a) The order shall:

1. Set the date and time for hearing on the order to show cause. However, the date for the hearing may not be set sooner than 20 days after the service of the order. When service is obtained by publication, the date for the hearing may not be set sooner than 30 days after the first publication. The hearing must be held within 60 days after the date of service. Failure to hold the hearing within such time does not affect the validity of the order to show cause or the jurisdiction of the court to issue subsequent orders.

2. Direct the time within which service of the order to show cause and the complaint must be made upon the defendant.

3. State that the filing of defenses by a motion or by a verified or sworn answer at or before the hearing to show cause constitutes cause for the court not to enter the attached final judgment.

4. State that the defendant has the right to file affidavits or other papers at the time of the hearing and may appear personally or by way of an attorney at the hearing.

5. State that, if the defendant files defenses by a motion, the hearing time may be used to hear the defendant's motion.

6. State that, if the defendant fails to appear at the hearing to show cause or fails to file defenses by a motion or by a verified or sworn answer or files an answer not contesting the foreclosure, the defendant may be considered to have waived the right to a hearing and in such case the court may enter a final judgment of foreclosure ordering the clerk of the court to conduct a foreclosure sale.

7. State that if the mortgage provides for reasonable attorney's fees and the requested attorney's fees do not exceed 3 percent of the principal amount owed at the time of filing the complaint, it is unnecessary for the court to hold a hearing or adjudge the requested attorney's fees to be reasonable.

8. Attach the final judgment of foreclosure the court will enter, if the defendant waives the right to be heard at the hearing on the order to show cause.

9. Require the mortgagee to serve a copy of the order to show cause on the mortgagor in the following manner:

a. If the mortgagor has been served with the complaint and original process, service of the order may be made in the manner provided in the Florida Rules of Civil Procedure.

b. If the mortgagor has not been served with the complaint and original process, the order to show cause, together with the summons and a copy of the complaint, shall be served on the mortgagor in the same manner as provided by law for original process.

Any final judgment of foreclosure entered under this subsection is for in rem relief only. Nothing in this subsection shall preclude the entry of a deficiency judgment where otherwise allowed by law.

(b) The right to be heard at the hearing to show cause is waived if the defendant, after being served as provided by law with an order to show cause, engages in conduct that clearly shows that the defendant has relinquished the right to be heard on that order. The defendant's failure to file defenses by a motion or by a sworn or verified answer or to appear at the hearing duly scheduled on the order to show cause presumptively constitutes conduct that clearly shows that the defendant has relinquished the right to be heard. If a defendant files defenses by a motion or by a verified or sworn answer at or before the hearing, such action constitutes cause and precludes the entry of a final judgment at the hearing to show cause.

(c) In a mortgage foreclosure proceeding, when a default judgment has been entered against the mortgagor and the note or mortgage provides for the award of reasonable attorney's fees, it is unnecessary for the court to hold a hearing or adjudge the requested attorney's fees to be reasonable if the fees do not exceed 3 percent of the principal amount owed on the note or mortgage at the time of filing, even if the note or mortgage does not specify the percentage of the original amount that would be paid as liquidated damages.

(d) If the court finds that the defendant has waived the right to be heard as provided in paragraph (b), the court shall promptly enter a final judgment of foreclosure. If the court finds that the defendant has not waived the right to be heard on the order to show cause, the court shall then determine whether there is cause not to enter a final judgment of foreclosure. If the court finds that the defendant has not shown cause, the court shall promptly enter a judgment of foreclosure.

(2) In an action for foreclosure, other than residential real estate, the mortgagee may request that the court enter an order directing the mortgagor defendant to show cause why an order to make payments during the pendency of the foreclosure proceedings or an order to vacate the premises should not be entered.

(a) The order shall:

1. Set the date and time for hearing on the order to show cause. However, the date for the hearing shall not be set sooner than 20 days after the service of the order. Where service is obtained by publication, the date for the hearing shall not be set sooner than 30 days after the first publication.

2. Direct the time within which service of the order to show cause and the complaint shall be made upon the defendant.

3. State that the defendant has the right to file affidavits or other papers at the time of the hearing and may appear personally or by way of an attorney at the hearing.

4. State that, if the defendant fails to appear at the hearing to show cause and fails to file defenses by a motion or by a verified or sworn answer, the defendant may be deemed to have waived the right to a hearing and in such case the court may enter an order to make payment or vacate the premises.

5. Require the mortgagee to serve a copy of the order to show cause on the mortgagor in the following manner:

a. If the mortgagor has been served with the complaint and original process, service of the order may be made in the manner provided in the Florida Rules of Civil Procedure.

b. If the mortgagor has not been served with the complaint and original process, the order to show cause, together with the summons and a copy of the complaint, shall be served on the mortgagor in the same manner as provided by law for original process.

(b) The right to be heard at the hearing to show cause is waived if the defendant, after being served as provided by law with an order to show cause, engages in conduct that clearly shows that the defendant has relinquished the right to be heard on that order. The defendant's failure to file defenses by a motion or by a sworn or verified answer or to appear at the hearing duly scheduled on the order to show cause presumptively constitutes conduct that clearly shows that the defendant has relinquished the right to be heard.

(c) If the court finds that the defendant has waived the right to be heard as provided in paragraph (b), the court may promptly enter an order requiring payment in the amount provided in paragraph (f) or an order to vacate.

(d) If the court finds that the mortgagor has not waived the right to be heard on the order to show cause, the court shall, at the hearing on the order to show cause, consider the affidavits and other showings made by the parties appearing and make a determination of the probable validity of the underlying claim alleged against the mortgagor and the mortgagor's defenses. If the court determines that the mortgagee is likely to prevail in the foreclosure action, the court shall enter an order requiring the mortgagor to make the payment described in paragraph (e) to the mortgagee and provide for a remedy as described in paragraph (f). However, the order shall be stayed pending final adjudication of the claims of the parties if the mortgagor files with the court a written undertaking executed by a surety approved by the court in an amount equal to the unpaid balance of the mortgage on the property, including all principal, interest, unpaid taxes, and insurance premiums paid by the mortgagee.

(e) In the event the court enters an order requiring the mortgagor to make payments to the mortgagee, payments shall be payable at such intervals and in such amounts provided for in the mortgage instrument before acceleration or maturity. The obligation to make payments pursuant to any order entered under this subsection shall commence from the date of the motion filed hereunder. The order shall be served upon the mortgagor no later than 20 days before the date specified for the first payment. The order may permit, but shall not require the mortgagee to take all appropriate steps to secure the premises during the pendency of the foreclosure action.

(f) In the event the court enters an order requiring payments the order shall also provide that the mortgagee shall be entitled to possession of the premises upon the failure of the mortgagor to make the payment required in the order unless at the hearing on the order to show cause the court finds good cause to order some other method of enforcement of its order.

(g) All amounts paid pursuant to this section shall be credited against the mortgage obligation in accordance with the terms of the loan documents, provided, however, that any payments made under this section shall not constitute a cure of any default or a waiver or any other defense to the mortgage foreclosure action.

(h) Upon the filing of an affidavit with the clerk that the premises have not been vacated pursuant to the court order, the clerk shall issue to the sheriff a writ for possession which shall be governed by the provisions of s. 83.62.

History.--s. 14, ch. 93-250; s. 3, ch. 2001-215.

ABOUT THE AUTHOR

Jeffrey Smith is currently a licensed Realtor and licensed Mortgage Broker.

Shortly after graduating from Florida State University Jeff obtained his first real estate license in 1976 and began selling full time in the Orlando area. Many years passed and one of his moves was to Lake County in 2004. (About 30 miles NW of Orlando) When the economy changed in 2007, he saw the "writing on the wall" and began to deal strictly with homeowners that were about to lose their homes. Along with his wife, Gail, (also a licensed Realtor) they live and work in Lake County, Florida.

To Contact Jeff by e-mail:

AvoidFloridaForeclosure@gmail.com